CHANITA R. RAMSEY

Unchained: The Awakening of the
Empath's Soul

INSPIRED
BY LOVE & GRACE
PUBLISHING

Dedication:

To every woman who has poured out her heart only to feel empty,
To every empath who has been silenced, manipulated,
or broken by those who could not love rightly,
To every soul who is walking through the fire of betrayal, pain, and isolation—
This book is for you.
May you find solace in these pages, clarity in your journey,
and the courage to rise into the freedom God has already prepared for you.

Contents

Acknowledgments

First and foremost, I thank God for His unfailing love, guidance, and patience in my journey. Every tear, every moment of brokenness, and every season of silence was met with His quiet but powerful presence.

To the women who have shared their stories, struggles, and hearts with me—you have inspired every word in this book. Your courage fuels this ministry.

To my family, my children, and my supporters—you reminded me daily of the strength of love and the power of faith.

And finally, to every empath who reads this book: may you know that your sensitivity is not a weakness, your love is not a burden, and your soul is divinely equipped to soar.

Introduction

The Chains That Tried tio Break Me

I want to begin by telling you something very important: I am not writing this book from a place of perfect victory. I am not standing at the finish line with all the answers neatly folded and wrapped. I am writing this from the battlefield, from the trenches where the struggle is real, the tears are fresh, and the questions still linger.

If you've ever loved a narcissist, you know what I mean. You know the hunger — the craving for their attention, their approval, their love — and how that craving can quietly, painfully consume you. You've poured out your heart, your time, your energy, your very self, and often, it felt like nothing was ever enough. You've begged, prayed, and hoped that somehow, love alone could heal them, fix them, make them see you, honor you, or change.

I've been there too. And I want you to know something that may feel hard to believe right now: the chains that tried to break you... those very chains are the ones God is using to awaken you.

I know what it feels like to be drained, to feel unseen, to wonder if your heart will ever recover from the emotional weight you've carried. I know what it feels like to pray for rescue and feel only silence. I know the nights when the tears are endless, and the mornings come, but your soul feels stuck, heavy, and defeated.

But here's the truth: God sees every tear. God hears every cry. God was never absent. He allowed the breaking, not to punish you, but to awaken you. He allowed the pain not to destroy you, but to reveal to you your own strength, your own value, your own soul's calling.

This book is written for the empath who has loved too much, given too much, and yet still longs for freedom. It is written for you — the one who is asking the same questions I've asked myself:

Why me? Why this pain? Will I ever be whole again?

I am walking this journey with you. Together, we will explore the hunger that keeps us bound, the bond that traps us, the disruption that opens our eyes, the awakening that sets us free, and the paradigm shift that God orchestrates when we finally let go and rise.

By the end of this book, I pray you will see the chains for what they really are: not the end of your story, but the beginning of your freedom. You are not defeated. You are awakening. You are unchained.

I

Part One – The Hunger (sets up the empath's lens)

Chapter 1: The Drug of Affirmation

Why the Empath Craves the Attention and Love-Bombing of a Narcissist

Dear one,

I see you. I see the way your heart has poured endlessly into someone who could never meet you where you are. I see the sleepless nights you spent hoping, praying, and believing that your love could fix, heal, or awaken them. I see the tears you've hidden, the silence you've endured, the quiet ache in your chest that no one else seems to notice.

You gave. And gave. And gave again.

And yet, somehow, it was never enough.

You were drawn in by the brilliance of their attention, the intoxicating rush of their praise, the warmth of their affection. At first, it felt like magic. Every thoughtful word, every compliment, every gesture—small or grand—stirred something inside you that had been longing for years to feel seen, cherished, and desired.

That attention, that love-bombing, was like a drug.

And I don't say that lightly. Because I know how hard it is to stop craving it, even when your heart already knows it's not healthy. For an empath, love is life. You give because it's who you are. You pour because your soul recognizes need. You nurture because you feel. And you hope because hope is embedded deep in your bones.

But the truth is, the person you gave to could not sustain your love. They could not receive your heart as it was meant to be received. And that, my dear, was never a reflection of your worth.

The empath's hunger is not a weakness—it is a testament to how profoundly you can love. It is a sign of your depth, your sensitivity, your soul's capacity for connection. But when that gift is placed in the hands of someone who cannot cherish it, the pain is undeniable. You begin to wonder if your heart was too much, too tender, too giving. You question yourself. You ask God, Why does it hurt so much to give what I was born to give?

And here is the mercy in this moment: God sees every ounce of love you offered. He watches every tear you shed. He counts every prayer whispered in the dark. The love you gave, even if it felt wasted, was never lost. It was always planting seeds in your soul—seeds of awakening, seeds of clarity, seeds of strength you have yet to fully realize.

You are allowed to grieve the love that was never returned. You are allowed to mourn the emptiness where you expected fullness. You are allowed to feel the sting of giving your all and receiving so little in return. These feelings are sacred—they are the raw material God uses to shape your heart into something unbreakable.

I want you to hear me clearly: it was never your fault. It was never because you loved too much or cared too deeply. It was because the person before you was not capable of receiving your love in the way your heart longed for. And now, by God's grace, you are beginning to see that this hunger, this ache, is not a trap—it is a calling.

Your love has always been a light. Even when it felt like it was swallowed by shadows, it remained bright. Now, it is time to turn that light inward, to feed the parts of yourself that were starved, to reclaim what was always yours: your peace, your joy, your heart, fully intact and unapologetic.

You are not broken. You are not too much. You are not a failure because they could not love you in return. You are awakening. And in this awakening, you will learn that the love you have been giving so freely is not meant to be trapped in someone else's hands—it is meant to flow from you, for you, and through you into the world God has prepared for you.

Take a deep breath, dear one. Let yourself feel the weight of your giving, and let yourself also feel the power of your soul beginning to rise. You have survived the hunger, the emptiness, the one-sided love. And now, for the first time, you are learning what it means to give to yourself without apology.

Chapter 2: The Mirror Effect

How the Narcissist Exposes Hidden Wounds

Dear one,

Have you ever felt that pang of confusion when someone's words or actions strike you so deeply, it feels like they know your heart better than you do? That's not a coincidence. That's the mirror effect at work.

The narcissist, without even trying, holds up a reflection of your hidden wounds. The very parts of yourself you've buried, denied, or forgotten—the insecure corners, the doubts, the fears—suddenly stand exposed. Every insult, every subtle slight, every act of neglect or manipulation hits not just because of what they do, but because it echoes the places inside you that have been fragile for far too long.

You see, the empath's heart is tender and finely tuned. You feel deeply. You care intensely. And because of that sensitivity, the narcissist's behavior can pierce through the walls you've built around your pain and make you question your worth, your judgment, your value.

But here's the truth: what is being reflected to you is not who you are. It is what has always been there, waiting for acknowledgment and healing. The narcissist did not create your wounds—they merely held up a mirror, forcing you to see them. And while it feels painful, confusing, and unfair, this mirror is a gift in disguise.

I know how heavy this can feel. I know the nights when you replay conversations in your mind, wondering why their words cut so deeply, why their absence hurts so much, why you are always the one left aching. And I know the quiet shame that creeps in, the part of you that whispers, Maybe I am too much, maybe I am not enough.

Listen carefully: that whisper is a lie.

The truth is that your wounds were never weaknesses—they were invitations for growth. They were soft, vulnerable spaces in your heart that God intended to awaken you through. The narcissist, in all their chaos and deception, could not give you what you needed. But they did force you to confront what you had been avoiding: the areas in yourself that were waiting for love, for recognition, for compassion.

The mirror effect is not punishment. It is revelation. It is the divine uncovering of truth hidden beneath layers of survival, people-pleasing, and unhealed pain. What feels like attack is actually illumination. What feels like rejection is actually redirection. What feels like humiliation is actually an opportunity to reclaim your power.

This is where the empath begins to awaken. You start to see that every time you feel wounded by their words or actions, it is not about you being broken. It is about God revealing what needs care within your soul. And as you learn to pause, to breathe, and to reflect, the mirror becomes your teacher.

You are allowed to cry. You are allowed to feel the sting of recognition. You are allowed to grieve the parts of yourself that have been overlooked or dismissed. And in that grief, you will begin to see something extraordinary: your wounds are not permanent. They are not your shame. They are your path to awakening.

Take this moment, dear one, and look into the mirror the narcissist has placed before you. See the tender, beautiful, resilient heart that has survived the blows and betrayals. See the parts of yourself that long for love, for care, for recognition. And know this: God sees it too. He sees every hidden corner, every unspoken longing, every quiet ache. And He is beginning to show you how to heal it, to love it, and to use it as a light to guide your way forward.

Your pain is not the end of your story. It is the invitation to step deeper into your truth, to embrace your wholeness, and to rise from the mirror with clarity, courage, and a heart that knows its own value.

This is the awakening. This is the beginning of seeing yourself as God sees you: whole, worthy, and unbreakable.

Chapter 3: Starved Hearts

Why the Empath Keeps Giving Even When It's Draining

Dear Heart,

There is a kind of hunger that no amount of giving can ever satisfy. A hunger that makes you pour and pour until your soul feels like it's running dry. It whispers, If I just love a little more, if I just sacrifice a little harder, maybe this time he will see me, value me, choose me.

This is the hunger of a starved heart.

For the empath, giving is like breathing. You give because it feels natural, almost holy. You give because you believe love is the cure to every wound—yours and theirs. And when you meet a narcissist, that hunger collides with their emptiness in a way that feels electric, almost divine. You think, This is my purpose. I was made to love him back to life.

But here is the painful truth: what you thought was love was often bondage.

At first, it feels beautiful—your compassion is met with need, your presence is met with longing. But slowly, the cycle begins: you give, they take. You forgive, they wound again. You bend, they demand more. And somewhere in the middle, your love—so pure, so giving—becomes a cage.

You thought you were building intimacy, but you were building a prison.

Every time you excused their lies, you welded another bar to the cage. Every time you silenced your needs to meet theirs, you locked the door a little tighter. Every time you believed their empty promises, you handed them the key.

And yet... you kept giving.

Why? Because your heart is starved too. Not for their love—but for the love you have withheld from yourself. Deep down, you long for validation, affirmation, a reminder that you are enough. The narcissist exploits this hunger, feeding you crumbs of affection to keep you hooked while draining you of your very essence.

And so you stay. You give. You love. You pour. You ache.

But dear one, this is not love. This is survival disguised as devotion.

True love does not demand that you bleed yourself dry. True love does not silence your soul. True love does not hold you hostage in the name of sacrifice. What you have been calling love is really bondage, and the only way to be free is to recognize the cage for what it is.

This realization is not meant to shame you. It is meant to awaken you. Because once you see the cage, you can no longer unknow it. Once you see how your giving has been twisted against you, you can begin to take back your power.

Yes, your empathy is a gift. Yes, your compassion is holy. Yes, your heart is a well of healing. But it was never meant to be weaponized against you.

God never called you to destroy yourself in the name of saving someone else. That is not love—that is bondage. And it is not His will for you.

Your starved heart is not a curse. It is a compass. It is pointing you back to the source of love that never runs out, the one well that will never leave you empty: God's love. When you begin to drink from that well, you realize that you were never made to pour endlessly for someone who cannot hold what you give. You were made to overflow, not to be emptied.

Dear empath, hear this: you are not weak because you gave. You are not foolish because you stayed. You were hungry, and you fed the only way you knew how. But now your eyes are opening. Now you see that giving without receiving is not love, but bondage. And now you are being called higher—called to a love that heals you, fills you, and frees you.

This is the breaking of the cage. This is the moment you begin to see that your heart was never meant to starve.

You were meant to be full.

II

Part Two – The Bond (unpacking the dynamic)

Chapter 4: Feeding the Narcissist

The Empath's Addiction to Giving

There is a point in every empath's story where giving stops being a choice and starts becoming a compulsion. What once felt like love, service, and compassion slowly hardens into something else—something desperate. It becomes an addiction.

The narcissist knows this. In fact, he depends on it. He thrives because you feed him. And you keep feeding him because you believe, deep in your soul, that one day it will be enough—that one day he will finally look at you, see your worth, and choose you.

But that day never comes.

Instead, the more you give, the more he takes. And the more he takes, the smaller you become. This is the silent destruction—the unraveling of your voice, your identity, and your spirit.

The Silent Destruction

At first, it is subtle. You stop wearing the clothes he criticizes. You bite your tongue when he dismisses your opinion. You lower your voice when he mocks your excitement. Piece by piece, you learn to adjust, to shrink, to edit yourself.

Soon, you don't even recognize the woman in the mirror. She looks like you, but her fire has dimmed. Her laughter is quieter. Her eyes carry a heaviness that wasn't there before.

This is not coincidence. This is design.

The narcissist's goal is not just to take from you—it is to erase you. To hollow you out so that you exist only as a reflection of his needs, his wants, his desires. The louder his ego becomes, the quieter your soul grows.

This is what it means to be addicted to giving. You begin to pour until you are empty, and yet, you still reach for the cup—still trying to find one more drop, one more ounce of strength, one more way to keep him alive, even as you wither.

The Theft of Voice

Your voice is powerful—it carries truth, wisdom, and divine authority. But in the hands of a narcissist, your voice becomes a threat.

So he mocks it. He twists your words. He calls you "too sensitive," "too emotional," "too much." Soon, you begin to doubt yourself. Maybe you are too much. Maybe you are the problem. Maybe if you just stay quiet, things will be peaceful.

And so, you silence yourself. Not because you lack words, but because you have been conditioned to believe your words don't matter.

But here's the truth: the enemy was never after your love—it was after your voice. Because your voice is what carries your power. And if he can strip you of that, he can keep you in bondage.

The Assault on Identity

There is nothing more dangerous to a narcissist than a woman who knows who she is.

And so, he chips away at your identity. He rewrites your story with lies: You're nothing without me. You'll never find better. No one else could love you like I do. Slowly, his words replace your own. His definition of you becomes louder than your inner knowing.

The empath—so full of life, love, and possibility—begins to disappear.

What remains is a shell, desperate to keep the peace, desperate to keep the connection alive, desperate to hold on to a love that feels more like a leash.

The Crushing of Spirit

Perhaps the deepest wound of all is this: the attempt to kill your spirit.

You were born with light in your soul, fire in your bones, and a calling stamped on your life. But under the weight of his manipulation, that light feels dim. Your fire flickers. Your calling feels far away.

You begin to wonder if God has forgotten you. You begin to wonder if this is all there is—this cycle of giving and starving, pouring and emptying, hoping and despairing.

But here is the truth, dear heart: your spirit cannot be killed. Bruised? Yes. Weary? Yes. But destroyed? Never.

Because what the narcissist didn't know is that even in your emptiness, God was preserving a remnant. Even in your silence, He was writing a louder story. Even in your brokenness, He was preparing your awakening.

The Awakening Within the Bond

Addiction to giving feels unbreakable. But the moment you realize that your giving has not healed him—it has only harmed you—is the moment you begin to see the chains for what they are.

You cannot feed someone who only devours. You cannot heal someone who thrives on your bleeding. And you cannot call bondage "love" and expect it to transform.

The empath's awakening begins here: in the recognition that giving is beautiful when it flows from fullness, but deadly when it flows from emptiness. That your worth is not measured by how much you can sacrifice, but by the fact that you were created in the image of God—already enough, already chosen, already loved.

The narcissist tried to silence your voice, erase your identity, and crush your spirit. But instead, he awakened the warrior in you—the woman who now knows that she was never created to feed destruction.

You were created to nurture life.

You were created to reflect God's love.

You were created to soar.

And this bond, as painful and destructive as it has been, will become the holy disruption that teaches you the difference between love and bondage, giving and addiction, survival and freedom.

Dear empath, the bond may have wounded you, but it will not define you.

Your voice is rising again.

Your identity is returning.

Your spirit is unshakable.

You are awakening, even here.

Chapter 5: The Transaction Masquerading as Love

I t takes tremendous courage to admit this truth: what you thought was love was not love at all. It was survival.

The nights you stayed awake replaying his words, the mornings you woke up determined to try harder, the countless sacrifices you made—it all felt like love. You called it loyalty. You called it commitment. You called it "standing by your man."

But underneath those words was something darker: fear.

Fear of losing him. Fear of being abandoned. Fear of being unseen, unwanted, unworthy.

That fear is what kept you giving. That fear is what kept you silent. That fear is what made you believe that if you just endured long enough, eventually he would see your worth.

But love built on fear is not love. It is survival dressed in disguise.

The Illusion of Love

In the beginning, it seemed perfect. He mirrored back everything you longed for—attention, admiration, intimacy. It was intoxicating. He convinced you that what you had was rare, unmatched, destiny.

But slowly, the balance shifted. The attention waned. The admiration turned into criticism. The intimacy became conditional.

And yet, you stayed. Why? Because deep down, you were not chasing love anymore—you were chasing survival.

You needed him to stay, not because he was good for you, but because losing him felt like losing yourself. He became the source of your validation, the drug that quieted your hunger for worth. And so, even when he gave you crumbs, you convinced yourself it was a feast.

This is the cruelest illusion of all—that scarcity is love.

The Transaction of Pain

When you strip it bare, the empath–narcissist dynamic is a transaction:

- I will pour into you, if you promise not to leave me.
- I will silence myself, if you promise to stay.
- I will lose pieces of myself, if you promise to love me back.

Every gift of yourself came with an unspoken bargain. You did not give freely—you gave in hopes of being chosen. You gave in hopes of being seen. You gave in hopes that one day, he would finally repay your sacrifice with the love you were starving for.

But survival bargains never produce love. They only produce exhaustion.

Because no matter how much you gave, it was never enough. The transaction always left you depleted, while he walked away richer.

When Love Turns Into Fear

True love makes you feel safe. True love brings peace. True love strengthens your spirit.

But survival love does the opposite. It leaves you anxious, restless, always on edge. You never know which version of him you will get—the charming one who pulls you close or the cruel one who pushes you away.

So you learn to adapt. You learn to tiptoe. You learn to study his moods like a map, trying to predict and prevent the next explosion.

That is not love. That is bondage.

And yet, you stayed, because your nervous system had learned to confuse chaos with chemistry. Your spirit had learned to call suffering "sacrifice." Your heart had learned to call fear "love."

The Cost of the Bargain

The empath pays dearly for this transaction.

- Her joy grows dim.
- Her laughter fades.
- Her dreams gather dust.
- Her body carries the weight of stress and exhaustion.

And worst of all, her soul begins to whisper the lie: Maybe I am not enough. Maybe this is all I deserve.

But hear me, dear empath: that lie is not the end of your story.

Because God will never let the counterfeit outshine the real thing. He will never allow the illusion of love to satisfy you when He has designed you for the fullness of it.

The Holy Exposure

When the curtain falls and the illusion shatters, it feels like devastation. You mourn. You grieve. You ache with the realization that what you thought was love was a transaction for survival.

But in that devastation lies a holy exposure. God reveals the truth not to destroy you, but to awaken you.

He shows you the difference between fear and love, between bondage and freedom, between transaction and covenant. He reminds you that His love is not earned through survival—it is poured out freely, unconditionally, without bargains.

This is the turning point. This is where your spirit begins to breathe again.

Stepping Into True Love

The unraveling of the counterfeit makes room for the real.

- A love where your voice is heard.
- A love where your presence is cherished.
- A love where you are not surviving—you are thriving.

And it begins not with another relationship, but with the one you form with yourself and with God. The moment you stop bargaining for crumbs is the moment you start feasting on the love that has always been waiting for you.

Dear empath, survival is not your destiny. Transaction is not your portion. Fear is not your inheritance.

You were created for more.

You were created for love in its purest, holiest form.

And now, you are awakening to the truth that the counterfeit cannot hold you anymore.

Chapter 6: When Empathy Becomes a Cage

E mpathy is a beautiful gift. It is the ability to feel beyond yourself, to see into another's pain, to love without conditions. It is the heart of God reflected in human form.

But when placed in the hands of a narcissist, that very gift can become a prison.

Because the moment your empathy is twisted into obligation, manipulated into silence, or stretched beyond its limits—it ceases to feel like freedom. Instead, it becomes a cage.

The Gift That Turned Against You

You thought your compassion could heal him.

You thought your patience would inspire him to change.

You thought your loyalty would make him stay.

But the more you gave, the more he took. And the more he took, the smaller you became.

Your empathy—meant to be a light—was now being used against you as a leash. Every time you tried to pull away, guilt yanked you back. Every time you thought of leaving, pity whispered, "But who will love him if I don't?"

So you stayed. Not out of love, but out of bondage disguised as love.

The Silent Destruction

This is how empathy becomes a cage:

- You silence your needs because his always seem bigger.
- You excuse his cruelty because you can "see his wounds."
- You justify his betrayal because you "understand his pain."

And with each excuse, a piece of you quietly dies.

Your voice weakens. Your identity blurs. Your spirit bends under the weight of constant giving.

You tell yourself, "I'm just being selfless." But true selflessness doesn't destroy the self—it multiplies love in both directions. What you are experiencing is not selflessness. It is self-erasure.

And self-erasure is not holy. It is bondage.

How the Cage Was Built

The narcissist knows your empathy is your soft spot. He studies it, exploits it, and uses it as a trap.

- When you catch him in a lie, he reminds you of his "trauma."
- When you ask for more, he plays the victim, making you feel guilty for wanting too much.
- When you try to walk away, he cries, "You're abandoning me," knowing those words slice straight into your heart.

Piece by piece, the cage closes in. And the bars aren't forged from metal—they are forged from your own compassion.

That's why it feels impossible to leave. Because to step out of the cage feels, in some twisted way, like betraying your gift.

22

The Wake-Up Call

But here is the truth, dear empath: real empathy was never meant to enslave you.

If your empathy only flows one way—if it only ever empties you while filling another—it is not love. It is manipulation.

If your empathy requires you to constantly diminish yourself, it is not Christlike sacrifice. It is idolatry of someone else's brokenness at the expense of your own soul.

This is the wake-up call: your empathy was meant to set people free, not to keep you bound.

The Holy Exchange

God never asked you to chain yourself to someone else's healing. He asked you to love, yes—but love rooted in truth, not deception. Love that uplifts, not love that erases.

When Jesus gave Himself for the world, He did it once. It was finished. He did not stay on the cross endlessly for those who refused to change. He knew when His sacrifice had fulfilled its purpose.

And now He whispers to you: "Daughter, it is finished. Step out of the cage. Your empathy was never meant to be your prison."

Breaking the Cage

The bars begin to break the moment you realize this: your empathy is not a weakness. It is a strength that was misused.

And the moment you redirect that empathy inward—toward yourself—you begin to heal.

- You begin to feel worthy of your own compassion.
- You begin to listen to your own needs with the same tenderness you gave him.

- You begin to see yourself through God's eyes—not as a savior of broken men, but as a beloved daughter who deserves peace.

This is not selfishness. This is freedom.

Your Empathy, Restored

One day, your empathy will no longer feel like a cage. It will feel like wings.

Wings that allow you to love without losing yourself.

Wings that allow you to give without emptying your soul.

Wings that carry you into relationships that honor your heart instead of devouring it.

You are not broken for having loved too much. You are not weak for having given too long. You are not foolish for having stayed too deep.

You were simply caged. And now, by God's grace, you are learning how to be free.

Your empathy is not your prison. It is your power. And once restored, it will become the very thing that propels you into your purpose.

III

Part Three – The Disruption (God steps in)

Chapter 7: The Holy Disruption

There comes a moment when everything shatters.

The mask slips. The lies unravel. The love you thought was unshakable crumbles beneath your feet. And as the dust settles, you are left broken, gasping, asking the same haunting question:

"God, why didn't You stop this?"

You prayed for rescue. You begged for the relationship to be restored. You cried for God to change him, to soften his heart, to make him finally see the love you were pouring out. But instead of a miracle, you got devastation.

And it feels like betrayal. Not just from the narcissist—but from God Himself.

When God Allows the Breaking

It is here, in this sacred space of heartbreak, that a deeper truth is revealed: God did not abandon you. He allowed the breaking because the bond itself was the prison.

You prayed for deliverance, but He knew that the only way out was through the wreckage.

You asked Him to fix the relationship, but He knew healing meant letting it collapse.

You begged Him to silence the pain, but He chose to let the pain awaken you.

This is the holy disruption.

It is not punishment. It is not cruelty. It is mercy disguised as loss.

Because the very thing that you thought was destroying you was actually the hand of God setting you free.

The Silence That Speaks

In those moments, God often feels silent. The heavens seem closed, your prayers feel unanswered, and you wonder if He has turned His face away.

But silence is not absence. Silence is often strategy.

Think of a surgeon who, mid-operation, does not pause to explain every cut. His silence does not mean neglect—it means precision. He is cutting to heal, not to harm.

In the same way, God's silence in the breaking is not His rejection. It is His scalpel. He is removing what could not go with you into your future.

The Disruption as Mercy

What if the very thing you thought was killing you was actually saving you?

- If God had answered your prayers to keep him, you would have remained bound.
- If God had softened his heart before you awakened, you would have stayed asleep.
- If God had made the narcissist "better," you would have continued to neglect your own healing.

The disruption, painful as it is, is God's mercy in disguise. It is His way of saying, "Daughter, I cannot let you live in chains. Even if I have to break your heart to save your soul, I will."

When Love Refuses to Let You Stay

This is not the love of a cruel God. This is the love of a jealous Father who refuses to let His daughter remain in bondage.

He loves you too much to let you keep drinking poison.

He loves you too much to let your empathy be wasted on someone who cannot receive it.

He loves you too much to let you die in a relationship that was never meant to define you.

So He disrupts it. Violently. Suddenly. Irrevocably.

Not because He wants to hurt you—but because He wants to heal you.

The Birth in the Breaking

Every breaking carries within it the seed of a new birth.

Yes, the breaking stripped you. Yes, it felt like death. But within the ashes, something holy is emerging: the real you.

The empath who no longer gives from starvation but from fullness.

The daughter who no longer seeks validation from man but receives it from God.

The soul who no longer lives in a cage but spreads her wings into freedom.

This is why the disruption had to come. Because without it, you would have never seen who you truly are.

An Invitation, Not Just a Loss

The holy disruption is not just an ending—it is an invitation. An invitation to know God in a way you never have before. An invitation to see yourself through His eyes, not through the broken mirror of a narcissist.

It is the beginning of your awakening.

And even though you may not see it yet, one day you will look back and whisper through tears of gratitude:

"It hurt, but it saved me. It broke me, but it built me. It disrupted me, but it delivered me."

Your Heart's Whisper

Dear empath, if you are in the middle of the breaking, hold on. God is not cruel. He is not careless. He is not ignoring you.

He is disrupting the very thing that tried to cage you. And though it feels unbearable now, this disruption is the sound of your chains falling.

This is not the end of your story.

This is the holy disruption that awakens your soul.

Chapter 8: The Silence of God

There is a silence that shakes the soul.

It comes after the breaking, when the storm has ripped through your life and left nothing but ruins behind. You stand there, raw and aching, waiting for God to swoop in with answers, comfort, or rescue. But instead of His voice, you hear nothing.

The heavens feel closed. The prayers echo back unanswered. The silence stretches so wide that it feels unbearable.

And in that silence, a whisper rises inside you: "God, have You abandoned me too?"

When Silence Feels Like Rejection

For the empath who has poured her whole heart into others, silence feels like punishment. You gave, you served, you loved until you had nothing left—yet now, when you need Him most, God seems quiet.

It's easy to confuse His silence with His absence. To believe the lie that because He hasn't spoken, He isn't there. To assume that because He hasn't moved, He doesn't care.

But beloved, silence is not rejection. Silence is a sanctuary.

The Wilderness of Isolation

God often leads His daughters into wilderness seasons where the noise is stripped away, where familiar voices disappear, and where the comfort of constant affirmation is removed.

Why?

Because in the wilderness, you learn to hear Him differently. Not in the thunder. Not in the applause. Not in the voice of the narcissist who once dictated your worth. But in the stillness.

The silence is not God's abandonment—it is His invitation. He is saying, "Daughter, come closer. Listen not with your ears, but with your spirit. Feel Me in the quiet. Find Me in the stillness."

I See You in the Silence

When you feel invisible, God leans in and whispers, "I see you."

When your tears fall unnoticed by others, He counts every drop.

When your prayers feel unanswered, He is storing them in heaven.

When you feel unseen, He is holding you in the palm of His hand.

Silence does not mean unseen. Silence means hidden—for protection, for preparation, for transformation.

Shattered, Yet Seen

You may feel shattered beyond repair. The pieces of your heart scattered in ways you don't believe can ever be mended. But God specializes in mosaics—He takes the fragments, the broken shards, and creates something even more beautiful than before.

The silence is not because He is ignoring you. It is because He is crafting something in you. Strength. Depth. A voice that is no longer silenced by the narcissist or shackled by codependency.

In this silence, He is birthing the woman who will rise.

When Silence Becomes Strength

There is a paradox hidden in this journey: the silence that once felt unbearable becomes the soil of your greatest strength.

- In the silence, you learn to trust God without needing constant confirmation.
- In the silence, you discover your identity is not tied to anyone else's voice but His.
- In the silence, you find that you are never truly alone.

The silence that once felt like abandonment will become the testimony of your awakening.

The Awakening in the Quiet

Beloved, the silence is not a punishment. It is the pause before the resurrection. It is the breath before the song. It is the stillness before the dawn breaks.

God has not abandoned you. He is closer than He has ever been.

He is saying: "I see you. I am with you. I am making you new."

And though you may not feel it yet, this silence is awakening your soul.

Chapter 9: The Exposure

The Breaking Was the Making

The exposure is never gentle. It doesn't arrive with a neat explanation or a quiet reveal. It comes like a storm—loud, undeniable, and devastating. The veil is ripped away, and you see him for who he truly is: not the savior you longed for, but the mirror of your hidden wounds.

At first, it feels unbearable. To realize that the love you gave so freely was not cherished but consumed. To face the truth that the arms you ran into for safety were the very arms that wounded you. The empath's heart breaks here, not just because of the narcissist's betrayal, but because of the illusion that dies with it.

But in the breaking comes the making.

It is here, in the ashes of deception, that God begins to lift your eyes. What you thought would destroy you becomes the very place where He breathes new life. The downfall of the narcissist, the exposure of his masks, becomes the mirror where you finally see yourself clearly. And what you see is not just your brokenness—it is your beauty, your strength, and your worth that somehow survived it all.

The Paradigm Shift: Chains No Longer Hold

The paradigm shift is not one single moment; it is a holy unfolding. It begins when you stop asking, "Why did this happen to me?" and start whispering, "Maybe it happened for me."

This shift is when survival gives way to awakening. When you realize that what you thought was love was really bondage. That the ties that pulled you back to him again and again were not sacred—they were soul chains forged in pain, trauma, and false promises.

And then, one day, the shift happens. The soul ties break.

It doesn't always happen loudly. Sometimes it's in the silence, in the stillness, when you feel God reaching into the deepest places of your heart. The cords loosen. The lies lose their grip. And what you thought you could never walk away from becomes the very thing you no longer crave.

This is freedom. Not because the narcissist changed, but because you did.

The paradigm shift is when you stop needing his validation because you've discovered your worth in the One who never lies, never abandons, never withholds His love. It's when your soul remembers:

- You were never created to be his supply.
- You were never born to be his savior.
- You were never meant to be consumed—you were meant to be cherished.

What was once a cage is now a testimony. What once silenced you now amplifies your voice. What once made you feel invisible now becomes the very platform where God declares: "I see you. I have always seen you."

The Breaking of the Soul Ties

The hardest part of this shift is not letting go of him—it's letting go of the version of yourself you thought you had to be to keep him.

The empath has spent years shrinking, pouring, bending, and breaking in order to hold a love that was never real. And when God breaks the soul tie,

He doesn't just free you from the narcissist—He frees you from that false self.

No more chains around your voice.

No more chains around your joy.

No more chains around your destiny.

You may have walked into the relationship chained, but you are walking out unchained. What the enemy meant to silence will now roar. What he tried to kill will now live stronger. What he thought he destroyed will now soar higher than ever before.

And when you look back, you will realize the truth: the exposure was not your ending—it was your beginning.

A Love Letter from God

My Beloved Daughter,

I know how heavy your heart has been. I saw every tear you cried in silence. I heard every prayer you whispered when you thought I was far away. I was never absent—I was working in the unseen, breaking chains you could not see.

You thought you lost everything, but what you lost was only what was never meant to remain. You thought you were abandoned, but I was holding you closer than ever. You thought you were forgotten, but I was writing a new story over your life—a story of freedom, healing, and wholeness.

You are not broken beyond repair. You are not invisible. You are not unworthy of love. You are Mine—chosen, cherished, and seen.

The chains that once bound you are falling now. The soul ties that drained you are cut by My hand. The identity that was stolen from you is being restored. You will rise, not as the woman you were, but as the woman I have called you to be—stronger, wiser, freer, radiant with My glory.

So breathe, Daughter. The worst is behind you. The shift has come. This is not the end—it is the beginning. Walk unchained. Walk awakened. Walk free.

With everlasting love,

Your Father

IV

Part Four – The Awakening (healing and transformation)

Chapter 10: Sacrificial vs. Self-Destructive Love

Declaring Liberty Over the Empath's Soul

Freedom does not arrive quietly—it rises within like a song long silenced, now finding its voice. The empath begins to whisper words she never thought she could say: "I am free. I am no longer bound. I am no longer giving my life away to prove my worth."

For years, she confused sacrificial love—the pure love that mirrors Christ's heart—with self-destructive love, the kind that empties without return, that bends until it breaks, that dies a little more each day in the name of "keeping the peace."

But God is not cruel, and His design for love was never meant to crush you. His love sets free—it does not cage. His love heals—it does not deplete. His love builds up—it does not strip away identity.

The Awakening of True Love

Sacrificial love is holy. It is the kind of love that Jesus displayed, a love that gives from a place of abundance, anchored in the Father. It pours out but never leaves you bankrupt, because it flows from God's endless supply.

Self-destructive love, on the other hand, is a counterfeit. It asks you to abandon yourself, silence your voice, and trade your joy for someone else's survival. It leaves you gasping for air, trapped in a cycle of pouring and never receiving.

The empath's awakening begins with this recognition: not every kind of giving is godly, and not every form of sacrifice is holy. Love that demands your destruction is not love at all—it is bondage dressed as devotion.

Declaring Liberty

Here is where the shift happens. The empath begins to stand tall, no longer bent beneath the weight of chains. She opens her mouth, and for the first time, she declares liberty over her soul.

- I will no longer confuse sacrifice with self-neglect.
- I will no longer believe love means losing myself.
- I will no longer shrink to make others feel bigger.
- I will love, but I will not be consumed.

These declarations are not wishful thinking—they are chains breaking. They are heaven echoing back: "Whom the Son sets free is free indeed."

Every empath must arrive at this sacred place, where she looks at her reflection and realizes: I am worthy of love that does not destroy me. I am worthy of peace that does not cost my soul. I am worthy of joy that does not require my silence.

The Liberty of Boundaries

Freedom does not mean the empath stops loving—it means she learns how to love without losing herself. Boundaries are not walls that keep people out; they are gates that protect the garden God planted within.

The empath learns that "no" can be holy, that rest is worship, and that protecting her heart is not selfish but sacred. She begins to understand that real love doesn't demand she be smaller—it celebrates her fullness.

And as she embraces this, her soul rises. She begins to walk lighter. Her laughter returns. Her tears, once bitter, become healing. The empath who once begged for scraps now feasts at the table of God's abundance.

A Song of Liberty

If you are here, at this chapter, this is your moment to sing a new song over your soul. Let these words rise from the ashes of your pain:

I am free.

I am loved.

I am chosen.

I am whole.

I am no longer chained to counterfeit love.

I belong to the God who gives me life, joy, and peace.

And I will love—but I will love as one who is free.

This is not just survival—it is resurrection. The empath is no longer a prisoner of her own giving. She is now a vessel of sacred love, poured out by God, but never emptied by man.

Chapter 11: When Silence Becomes Strength

No More Chains—She is Free

Silence once felt like death to the empath.

It was the loudest ache, the void that screamed, "You are forgotten, unseen, unloved." It was in the silence that she felt most abandoned—by him, by the world, even by God. Yet what she did not realize then was that silence was not her executioner. Silence was her midwife.

It was in the silence that her rebirth began.

The empath's turning point does not come in the noise of confrontation or the chaos of broken promises. It comes in the holy stillness where God strips away every voice but His own. No more lies. No more manipulation. No more apologies laced with deception. Just silence—pregnant with the sound of chains breaking.

And suddenly, she realizes: I am still here. I am still breathing. And I no longer need permission to exist.

Breathing Without Permission

For so long, she lived like her breath depended on him. The rise and fall of her chest was tethered to his approval, his attention, his validation. Every inhale begged, "Please don't leave me." Every exhale whispered, "Maybe this time he'll see me."

But the turning point comes when she inhales and realizes the oxygen is hers. She exhales and feels the weight lift. She does not need permission to take up space, to dream, to live, to laugh again.

This is when silence shifts from punishment to power.

It becomes the soil where she plants herself and finally grows—not as a shadow of someone else's desires, but as the radiant soul God always intended her to be.

From Bitter to Better

The choice stands before her like a fork in the road: bitterness or better.

Bitterness would be easy. After all, the wounds are deep. The betrayal is real. The scars on her heart tell the story of love that was more like captivity. But bitterness is another chain—and she has already learned what it feels like to live bound.

So she chooses better. Not because he deserves her forgiveness, but because she deserves her freedom.

Choosing better looks like releasing the need to rehearse the pain. It looks like trading the identity of "victim" for the destiny of "victor." It looks like standing in front of the mirror, not searching for what is broken, but blessing what is being healed.

Loving Herself the Way She Once Loved Him

The empath's greatest shift is not in how she views him, but in how she views herself.

For years, she poured rivers of love into the desert of his soul. She sacrificed her own joy, her own health, her own peace, just to keep him from running dry. But now—now the rivers turn inward. Now she waters her own soul with the same passion once wasted on his drought.

And as she loves herself, she discovers something breathtaking: self-love is not selfish. It is sacred. It is survival. It is worship.

By cherishing the woman God created her to be, she finally honors the Giver of life Himself.

The Declaration of Freedom

The empath rises. Not timid, not trembling, but steady. Chains lie shattered at her feet, their clinking no longer echoing in her ears. The silence that once suffocated her is now her anthem. It is the sound of peace.

She whispers to herself:

- I am free.
- I am loved.
- I am worthy.
- I am whole.

And with every declaration, she breathes deeper. Breathing without fear. Breathing without apology. Breathing without permission.

The turning point has come. She is not the same woman who bowed beneath the weight of his manipulation. She is the woman who rose.

No more chains.

No more cages.

No more captivity.

She is free.

A Prayer of Release

Father,

I lay down every chain that tried to hold me captive.

I release every voice that silenced me, every hand that broke me, and every lie that told me I was unworthy.

Today, I embrace Your silence—not as abandonment, but as the womb of my awakening.

I breathe in Your love, and I exhale the pain.

I breathe in freedom, and I exhale fear.

I breathe in worth, and I exhale shame.

From this moment forward, I will love myself with the same devotion I once poured into empty places.

I will guard my heart, not with walls of bitterness, but with rivers of Your truth.

I will rise—not as a victim, but as a victor.

No more chains.

No more cages.

No more captivity.

I am free, and my soul will sing of Your goodness forever.

Amen.

Chapter 12: The Empath's Calling

She Will Soar

Y ou made it through the breaking, the silence, the exposure, and the awakening. What once felt like the end was only the beginning. What you thought was death was really resurrection. What the enemy meant for evil, God has turned into a holy assignment.

You are not who you were when this journey began. The woman who poured herself out until she was empty has now learned to drink deeply from the living water. The woman who gave her love away without return has now discovered the greatest love—the love of God that heals, restores, and redefines.

This is not just survival; this is revival.

This is not just freedom; this is destiny.

This is not just healing; this is a holy calling.

The empathy inside of you is not a curse. It is a divine gift. A gift that once attracted brokenness now attracts purpose. A gift that once was used to drain you will now be used to overflow onto others. God did not create your heart to be trampled on—He created it to be a wellspring of life that points others to Him.

Loving Without Losing Yourself

The shift has happened. You no longer love from desperation, but from abundance. You no longer serve from lack, but from overflow. You no longer confuse sacrifice with self-destruction.

You now understand that your first calling is to love the Lord your God with all your heart, soul, and mind—and to love your neighbor as yourself. Notice: as yourself. God never asked you to erase yourself to love another. He asked you to honor Him by honoring the life He placed in you.

When you love yourself through God's eyes, you become unstoppable. You soar higher, because you are no longer weighed down by chains of shame, manipulation, or fear.

The Prophetic Declaration

Daughter, rise.

Step into the fullness of your calling.

Walk in the authority purchased for you by the blood of Jesus.

You are not broken—you are whole.

You are not silenced—you are a voice to nations.

You are not abandoned—you are chosen.

You are not forgotten—you are appointed for such a time as this.

Every chain that tried to bind you has become the evidence of your freedom. Every tear that fell in the silence has become a seed of joy that is now breaking forth. Every battle you thought would kill you has crowned you with victory.

The narcissist did not win. The pain did not win. The darkness did not win.

You rose. You lived. You soared.

And now—you are unchained.

You are called.

You are destined for greater.

The Empath's Ministry

From this day forward, your empathy becomes your ministry. Your compassion becomes your weapon. Your story becomes your testimony. You are no longer giving from a place of emptiness but from the overflow of God's Spirit within you.

You will be a voice for the silent.

You will be light in places where others see only darkness.

You will love—but you will love with wisdom, with boundaries, and with power.

God is raising you up, not just as an empath who survived, but as a prophetic voice who carries His heart to the world.

Benediction

And so, beloved, soar.
Soar into healing.
Soar into joy.
Soar into destiny.
For what tried to kill you has only awakened you.
What tried to silence you has only amplified you.
And what tried to chain you has only made you stronger.
You are free.
You are chosen.
You are loved.
You are unstoppable.
This is your calling. This is your rising. This is your time to soar.

Epilogue: Walking in Your Freedom

Beloved empath,

You have walked through the fire. You have faced the pain, the silence, the betrayal, and the awakening. And here you are—still standing, still breathing, still capable of loving, but now loving yourself first.

This is your moment. The chains that tried to bind you have fallen away. The weight of approval that once controlled you no longer dictates your worth. The voices that once questioned your value are silenced by the truth of who God says you are.

You are not broken. You are not defeated. You are a woman of strength, clarity, and divine purpose.

A Letter to Your Soul

D ear One,
I see you. I know the battles you fought silently, the nights you cried alone, and the moments you questioned if your heart would ever heal. I have been with you in every tear and every ache.

You gave and gave, often without receiving, and that is okay. Your love was not wasted—it was preparing you for a higher calling. Every moment you felt invisible, every time you wondered if it would ever be enough, God was shaping you into the woman who could walk in her authority, love without losing herself, and soar into her destiny.

Now, it is time to take your next step with courage. The past is behind you, the lessons are within you, and the future is calling your name.

Prophetic Declarations for the Empath

Speak these over yourself as you step into freedom:

- I am free from chains, bondage, and manipulation.
- I am whole, complete, and loved by God.
- I release every fear, every shame, and every lie the enemy tried to place on me.
- I walk in authority, clarity, and divine identity.
- I love without losing myself, I serve without depletion, and I live with passion and purpose.
- What tried to kill me only awakened me.
- I am unchained, called, and destined for greater.

Your Life Beyond This Book

This is not the end. It is the beginning of your next chapter—the chapter where you walk in clarity, live in joy, and minister through the gift of empathy God has placed in your heart.

Remember:

Your empathy is not a burden—it is your ministry.

Your scars are not shame—they are your testimony.

Your story is not over—it is only beginning to soar.

Take a deep breath, beloved. Feel the weight lift. Hear the voice of God saying: "Rise, daughter, and live in the fullness I created you for. You are mine, and you are unstoppable."